Looking Back

HISTORIC IMAGES OF NORTH CENTRAL CONNECTICUT

Volume 2 of 4

featuring historic images from
Manchester, Andover, Bolton, Coventry,
East Hartford and Hebron

Foreword and chapter introductions by
Richard Tambling

ACKNOWLEDGMENTS

The Journal Inquirer is pleased to present this first volume of "Looking Back: Historic Images of North Central Connecticut" — a collection of more than 250 pre-1950 photographs from the communities of Manchester, Andover, Bolton, Coventry, East Hartford and Hebron.

We would like to thank the many people and organizations who generously shared their photographs for this project. Without them, this book would not have been possible.

In addition to the generous contributions from Journal Inquirer readers, photographs were provided from the archives of several groups dedicated to preserving the history of this area. The participating organizations are:

Andover Historical Society

Bolton Town Clerk's Office

Connecticut Firemen's Historical Society Museum

Coventry Historical Society

East Hartford Historical Society

Hebron Historical Society

Manchester Historical Society

We would also like to thank Richard Tambling, editor of the Living section of the Journal Inquirer, for the time and effort he has put into this project. His knowledge of North Central Connecticut history and extensive contacts in the area have contributed greatly to the success of this endeavor.

TABLE OF CONTENTS

FOREWORD...4

VIEWS...5

SCHOOLS & EDUCATION.............................15

PUBLIC SERVICE 26

COMMERCE & INDUSTRY 39

FARM & HOME 63

PEOPLE...69

SOCIETY...81

TRANSPORTATION 89

DISASTERS 105

RECREATION & CELEBRATION 111

FOREWORD

The old photographs displayed on the pages of this book will fascinate and amaze many readers.

Most of the photos trigger the imagination. Some cause us to deconstruct modern landscapes so we can determine just where a road ran or a building stood. Others lead us to ponder the thoughts or feelings of an individual who died before we were born.

But there are some that were included simply because they are a joy to look at, offering a curious glimpse into times when life was markedly different than it is today; in some ways it was better, in some worse, but definitely unique from our point of view.

In this volume, we share images of six towns: Manchester, incorporated in 1823; Hebron, incorporated in 1708; East Hartford, incorporated in 1783; Coventry, incorporated in 1712; Bolton, incorporated in 1720; and Andover, incorporated in 1848.

In the photographs and captions in this book, you will encounter references to such historic factors as the once-thriving silk mills of Manchester and Coventry, the many mills and factories that made East Hartford prosper, and the agricultural heritage of Hebron, Bolton, and Andover.

The photos printed in this book, prepared by the Journal Inquirer, were gathered from the historical societies, museums, and library archives of our towns and loaned by individuals and local historians.

For their assistance, we are deeply grateful.

The Journal Inquirer hopes that readers will enjoy reading the book as much as we enjoyed creating it.

VIEWS

The wonderful thing about old photographs, like those contained in this book, is that they make the past accessible even to those of us with imaginations of limited strength.

Look at the turn-of-the-century East Hartford building depicted on this page. It dominates the scene and you can almost feel its sheer mass and solidity.

The same is true of many of the other structures displayed in the photos in this chapter.

Sadly, many of them no longer stand at their former locations in Manchester, Andover, Bolton, Coventry, East Hartford, and Hebron.

Time and the wrecking ball have swept them aside, and, for most of us, words alone can't resurrect them in our minds.

It's only through photographs like these that you can see and feel the influence that they exerted on the geography of our towns and on the people who went in and out of them and passed by them each day.

Village Street and Connecticut Boulevard, East Hartford, circa 1900. *Courtesy East Hartford Historical Society*

Cedar Swamp, Bolton, late 1800s. This became Bolton Lake, circa 1900. *Courtesy Bolton Town Clerk's Office*

Bird's-eye view of Manchester Green, taken from the hill behind Coburn house, site of present Baptist Church, early 1900s. *Courtesy Thelma Woodbridge*

School Street, Coventry, early 1900s. *Courtesy Coventry Historical Society, Ethel Crickmore Harris collection*

View of Main Street, Coventry, 1900.
Courtesy Coventry Historical Society,
A. Goodin Collection

Main Street, Coventry, 1890s. *Courtesy Bill Ayer*

A view of Manchester Green looking west including Old Woodbridge Tavern at the southwest corner of East Middle Turnpike and Woodbridge Street, 1910.
Courtesy Thelma Woodbridge

Street scene in East Hartford, early 1900s. *Courtesy East Hartford Historical Society*

Main Street, looking south, Coventry, early 1900s.
Courtesy Coventry Historical Society, Ethel Crickmore

Hartford Avenue, East Hartford, early 1900s. *Courtesy East Hartford Historical Society*

North Main Street looking west, Manchester, circa 1905. *Courtesy Morgan Campbell*

A Tradition of Caring and Community Pride

The original Manchester Memorial Hospital at the time of its dedication in 1921.

Manchester Memorial Hospital was built by a generous and resourceful community following a devastating health crisis – the great influenza epidemic of 1918. This plague affected an untold number of families in and around Manchester, and struck a quarter of the country's population, causing numerous deaths.

This event galvanized the community residents, who then rallied together to build a much-needed hospital. They raised $130,000 within a week, and the Cheney Brothers firm pledged an additional $65,000. That sum had the purchasing power of several million dollars today. The facility would serve both as a place to serve those needing critical medical care, and as a memorial to honor those who served this country in World War I, which had just ended.

A Board of Trustees was appointed to oversee the construction of the hospital and to govern it after it opened. In November of 1919, the cornerstone was laid, and the building was completed in a year. The doors of the hospital opened in 1920 at its current location on Haynes Street.

Today, Manchester Memorial Hospital is a thriving hospital that still has its roots in the community. Since 1995, it has been part of Eastern Connecticut Health Network, a non-profit health system that continues to be governed by residents, not corporate shareholders. Any funds left over from operations at the end of the year remain in the health system to purchase new equipment, improve facilities, and expand services.

As a full-service community hospital, Manchester Memorial offers the latest in advance medical technologies, and a full spectrum of services from birth to geriatric years. These include: comprehensive medical and surgical services; ambulatory surgery; a state-of-the-art emergency department; a walk-in medical center; diagnostic testing and treatment, including MRI and PET scanning capabilities; laser surgery; the Family Birthing Center for maternity services; a sleep disorders laboratory; extensive behavioral health services, on both an inpatient and outpatient basis; and, the John A. DeQuattro Community Cancer Center, which provides radiation therapy, chemotherapy, and surgical, medical, and other clinical and support services.

Community leaders gather for a groundbreaking ceremony for a building addition at the hospital in 1944.

Other affiliates of Eastern Connecticut Health Network include Rockville General Hospital, Woodlake at Tolland Health Care Center, and the Women's Center for Wellness in Vernon.

Manchester Memorial Hospital
71 Haynes Street, Manchester, CT 06040
(860) 646-1222

ECHN℠
Eastern Connecticut Health Network
The Communities' Choice℠ • www.echn.org

South Main Street, Hebron, circa, 1905. *Courtesy Hebron Historical Society*

Main Street and railroad crossing, North Manchester, 1906.
Courtesy Louis V. Mueller

Bird's-eye view of Andover, circa 1910. *Courtesy Andover Historical Society*

Street scene in Andover center, circa 1910. *Courtesy Andover Historical Society*

A view of a butcher shop and Bidwell Tavern in South Coventry, circa 1910. *Courtesy Coventry Historical Society*

Oakland Street, Manchester, circa 1915. *Courtesy Morgan Campbell*

Bolton center, circa 1915. *Courtesy Bolton Town Clerk's Office*

Street scene in Andover, 1915. *Courtesy Andover Historic Society*

SCHOOLS & EDUCATION

Modern readers may decide that many of the schoolhouses shown in the photographs in this chapter seem not merely quaint, but stunningly primitive.

Some of them didn't even have a bell hung up high to call in the pupils. The teacher had to use a hand-held model.

There's no denying that a two-room schoolhouse not even wired for electricity or equipped with indoor plumbing is a far cry from the institutions of today, with their libraries, computers, modern cafeterias, video equipment, and public address systems.

Of course, not all the institutions of the past that are shown here had multiple classes and a student body consisting of Tom Sawyers and Becky Thatchers crammed into rooms heated by pot-bellied stoves.

The more populated, more urban towns with more substantial funding behind them, like East Hartford and Manchester, were able to offer larger and better-equipped schools to their communities.

In the end, though, technology or no technology, the mission of all the schools you see here was precisely the same a few generations ago as it is today: to inspire and to educate the pupils and equip them to face life in an increasingly more sophisticated world.

Lincoln School (a Manchester elementary school) second grade students. Left to right, front row: Olive Finnegan Montovani, James Quish, Elsie McCormic, Francis Donahue, Alice Thresher, Naomi Campbell. Others unidentified.
Courtesy Olive Finnegan Montovani

Two-room Hebron Center School, circa 1882. *Courtesy Donald Robinson*

Burrows Hills School, circa 1895. Teacher was Eloise Ellis. Students are identified as: Bessie Peters (Long), Walter Wright, Emily Hanna (Lessard), Henry Andre, Edna Smith, Edward Smith. *Courtesy Hebron Historical Society*

Adelle White, teacher at Burrows Hills School, Hebron, late 1800s. *Courtesy Hebron Historical Society*

Hebron Select School students in 1906. Left to right, back row, Clifford Perry, Myron Post, Helen Foote, Robert Foote, Alphons Wright, James Clarke (teacher), Edward A. Smith, Clair Robinson, Della Frink, Elton Post, Elizabeth Porter, Everett Frink. Middle row, Genevieve Little, Leila Spencer, Florence E. Smith, Mabel Buell, Olive Smith, Rose Holbrook. Front row, Helen Lord, Annabelle Hannah, Ethel Porter, Dan Horton, Charlie Shikhetoff, Eleanor Lord. *Courtesy Clifford Wright*

Hebron Center School and Hebron Center students, circa 1941.
Courtesy Alberta Hilding

Silver Street School, Coventry, circa 1890. *Courtesy Coventry Historical Society*

Hebron Center School, 1926. *Courtesy Alberta Hilding*

Gilead Hill School students, circa 1894. *Courtesy Hebron Historical Society*

District No. 2 school on South Street, Coventry, 1920s. This school, now a residence, stands in N. Coventry at intersection of Cross and South streets. Left to right, back row, Edna Newell (Teacher), Christine Phillips, Clarence Bassett. Next row, Billy Phillip, Franklin Oakley, Howard Carpenter, Harry Smith, Wenifred Small, Viola Carpenter, Eva Vendeck. Front row, Jack Oakley, Robert Vendeck, _____ Vendeck, Robert Clock, Mildred Carpenter, Ruth Wright. *Courtesy Coventry Historical Society*

Children playing outside the Grammar School, Coventry, early 1900s. Edna Newell was the principal. *Courtesy Coventry Historical Society, Ethel Crickmore Harris collection*

Pond Hill School, across from the Prince of the Peace Church, Coventry, 1910. *Courtesy Bill Ayer*

Pond Hill School, Coventry, 1944. The children from the first and second grades are enjoying an International Day. *Courtesy Bill Ayer*

Center School on School Street, Coventry, circa 1920. Those in the photo include: Agnes Flaherty, Elizabeth Flaherty, Nettie Cour, Julia Flaherty, Humpy Flaherty, Nettie Moore Squires, May Clark, Ruby Higgins. The teacher was Edna Newell.
Courtesy Coventry Historical Society

Brick School students taught by Mrs. Evelyn Burdick, Coventry, 1941.
Courtesy Coventry Historical Society

Center Street School, Andover, circa 1903. *Courtesy Andover Historical Society*

Bolton school children, circa 1905. Those known, top row: Julius Strong, Ernest Strong, Mrs. Elizabeth White Finley, Miss Adelia N. Loomis. Second row, _____ Keeney Hutchinson, Carrie French Dietrichson. Third row, Lina Bidwell Roberts. Fourth row, Joseph Mack, Doris Warfield Manning, Margaret Daly, Kathering Vaughan, Elizabeth Daly, Mary Mathein Wippert. Front row, _____ Rose Franceschina, Helen Mathein. Seated is Maxwell Hutchinson. *Courtesy Eleanor and Norman Preuss*

South School or Center School, Bolton, 1912. Those known: Gladys Loomis, Evelyn Sarano, Peg Daly, Andrew Ansaldi, Rose Ansaldi, Dora Pinney, Arthur Pinney, Sarah Belle Pinney, Mike Sheridan and Clifford Loomis. *Courtesy Arlyne Ansaldi*

Center School, East Hartford, circa 1910. *Courtesy East Hartford Historical Society*

East Hartford High School, class of 1907. *Courtesy East Hartford Historical Society*

Manchester High School, South Manchester, circa 1920. The Teacher's Hall is the building at left. *Courtesy Morgan Campbell*

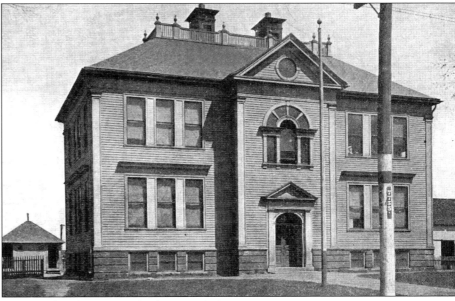

Union School, East Hartford, circa 1910. *Courtesy Louis V. Mueller*

East Hartford High School, circa 1920. *Courtesy Morgan Campbell*

Nathan Hale School class, Manchester, 1940. Jeanette Christine Richardson is sitting, fifth from left. *Courtesy Arlyne Ansaldi*

Graduating class of East Hartford High School, 1941. *Courtesy East Hartford Historical Society*

East Street School, eighth grade graduation class, 1941. *Courtesy Dorothy Wheelock*

The eighth grade graduation class, Manchester Green School, 1925. *Photo courtesy Thelma Woodbridge*

PUBLIC SERVICE

T he Manchester firehouse shown on this page looks today much as it did in the early 20th century, although in modern times, it's been reborn as the Connecticut Firemen's Historical Society Museum.

However, much of what's depicted in this chapter on public service looks very different from the way it used to and has changed dramatically.

Uniforms and equipment have been replaced with newer versions, while some of the buildings shown serve a new purpose nowadays or have been torn down.

And it's hard to imagine a modern postman handing the day's mail over to a family's dog, who races home and completes the delivery for him.

That moment, depicted in a 1917 Manchester photo, would have been a natural for Norman Rockwell to paint. However, it's as far removed from the 21st century as are the service-men wo are shown marching off to show a thing or two to Pancho Villa and the Kaiser or local kids gathering scrap metal to aid the war effort in the 1940s.

South Manchester Fire Department Hose and Ladder Company No. 1 on Pine Street with a 1921 Ahrens-Fox pumper truck and Torrent No. 1 from Norwich. The engine from Norwich was in Manchester for a parade. *Courtesy Connecticut Firemen's Historical Society Museum*

Manchester Green, late 1800s, looking east. The post office and general store are on the left followed by the Woodbridge house and followed by the Glastonbury Knitting Mill building.
Courtesy Thelma Woodbridge

Post office, Andover, circa 1900. *Courtesy Andover Historical Society*

MANCHESTER MEMORIAL HOSPITAL

Laying the cornerstone of Manchester Memorial Hospital was an impressive ceremony at which Manchester paid homage to its boys who gave their merry youth away for Country and for God, circa November 1919.

Companionship and pleasant diversions play an important role in getting well at the hospital, circa 1922.

A tree for each man who lost his life serving in World War I was planted along the front driveway of Manchester Memorial Hospital, circa 1920.

A baby is weighed in the hospital's nursery, circa 1923.

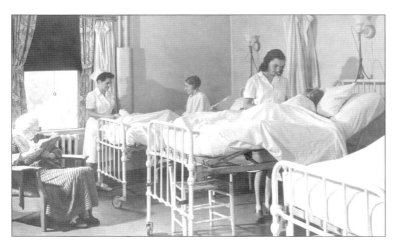

Patient ward at the hospital, circa 1938.

South Manchester Fire Department's 1907 hose and chemical wagon in front of the Pine Street fire station. *Courtesy Connecticut Firemen's Historical Society Museum*

Town hall, Andover, circa 1915. *Courtesy Andover Historical Society*

Public library in Hebron, circa 1910. *Courtesy Alberta Hilding*

Town meeting in Coventry, October 1, 1906. *Courtesy Andover Historical Society*

Wells Hall, East Hartford, circa 1907. *Courtesy East Hartford Historical Society*

South Manchester Fire Department Hose and Ladder Company No. 1 on Pine Street, circa 1913. This photo shows a 1912 Seagrave chemical truck, Chief Orion J. Atwood in his chief's car, a red runabout and a 1913 Seagrave ladder truck. *Courtesy Connecticut Firemen's Historical Society Museum*

Bolton Town Hall, shortly after it was built in 1914. *Courtesy Bolton Town Clerk's Office*

Store and post office, Manchester Green, circa 1915.
Photo courtesy Thelma Woodbridge

Company G First Connecticut Infantry was mobilized in 1916 for service in the Mexican Border Campaign. This photo was taken in front of their armory on Wells Street, Manchester, 1916. *Courtesy Norman Grimason*

South Manchester Fire Department Orford Hose Company No. 3 on Spruce Street. *Courtesy Manchester Historical Society*

Mr. Cornett, Manchester mailman, gives the mail to "Babe," Haeger's dog, to take home, 1917. *Courtesy Norman Grimason*

First Connecticut Infantry preparing to go to Arizona, circa 1916. Left to right: Unidentified, George Schiller, Annie Reichert Schiller, B. Schulz. *Courtesy Norman Grimason*

Company G, 102 Regiment leaves Manchester for France, 1917. *Courtesy Norman Grimason*

South Manchester Fire Department Center Hose Company No. 2 behind Center Congregational Church. This photo shows a 1912 White hose truck and a 1920 American LaFrance chemical and hose truck. *Courtesy Norman Grimason*

Post Mistress Alma Porter in front of the Hebron Post Office on the Green, circa 1939. *Courtesy Hebron Historical Society*

Community Hall, Grange Hall in the center of Bolton, 1930. It is now part of Town Hall. Also pictured is Bolton Congregational Church. *Courtesy Eleanor and Norman Preuss*

Proceeds of a scrap metal drive at the State Theater in Manchester, 1942. Fifth, from left is Jack Sanson, manager. *Courtesy Andrew Hall*

Group gathering at a War Bond Drive on Main Street, Manchester, opposite House and Hale's Department Store, 1942. *Courtesy Andrew Hall*

Navy Day on Main Street, Manchester, 1944. *Courtesy Andrew Hall*

Volunteers gather for Navy Day in Manchester, 1944. *Courtesy Andrew Hall*

March of Dimes drive at the State Theater, Manchester, 1945. *Courtesy Andrew Hall*

Manchester Police Department participates in a safe-driving campaign. *Courtesy Andrew Hall*

COMMERCE & INDUSTRY

In the next few pages, we are offered glimpses of some of the ways our grandparents and ancestors made their livings.

We see the wagons on which they delivered coal, meat, groceries, lumber, and even laundry, drawn by either oxen or horses.

We even see a company that made some of the wagons.

We also see mills where they sawed timber or made paper and other products. And we see the Cheney Brothers machine shop, which made the gears turn in the great silk mill.

We see downtown merchants and hotels, a filling station, saloons, and shops where they sold candy, hardware, or cut your hair.

Particularly interesting are the trades that have become virtually nonexistent today.

One of those was ice harvesting. In the days before freezers churned out cubes for us, we depended on nature for ice.

Blacksmithing is another nearly vanished trade depicted in the following pages.

And while some of us may well remember the days when milk was delivered to homes each morning, not many among us can recall the days when organ grinders and their monkeys were not an unheard-of sight.

Morton & Dwyer Company, early "discounters" on North Main Street, Manchester, early 1900s.
Courtesy Manchester Historical Society

Elwood Walker's sawmill on Woodbridge Farm near Vernon Street, Manchester, late 1800s. *Courtesy Thelma Woodbridge*

The Rose Block, Manchester, circa 1890. This was known as the finest block in Manchester. *Photo courtesy Charles Gilbert*

Hotel Andover on Center Street before it burned in 1916. *Courtesy Andover Historical Society*

Wesley Hollister, Coal and Masons' Supplies, located at the corner of Hilliard and Main streets, Manchester, late 1800s. *Courtesy Manchester Historical Society*

F.J. Olds meat delivery wagon, Bolton, circa 1905. *Courtesy Bolton Town Clerk's Office*

C.C. Graves Meat Company, refrigerator wagon, Coventry, late 1800s. *Courtesy Coventry Historical Society, Sterling MacPherson collection*

S.A. Doane store on Main Street, North Manchester early 1900s. *Courtesy Manchester Historical Society*

Paper mills in Andover, circa 1900. *Courtesy Andover Historical Society*

Workers outside a mill in Coventry, early 1900s. *Courtesy Coventry Historical Society*

E.A. Tracy Mill, Coventry, early 1900s. *Courtesy Coventry Historical Society, Ethel Crickmore Harris collection*

Henry Armstrong wagon company, South Coventry, circa 1900. *Courtesy Coventry Historical Society*

Cheney Bros. machine shop workers, Manchester, 1902. *Courtesy South Windsor Historical Society, Sally Edlund collection*

An early delivery truck manufactured by Henry Armstrong wagon company, South Coventry, circa 1900. *Courtesy Coventry Historical Society*

Ice harvesting was an important industry in Manchester in the early 1900s.
Courtesy Norman Grimason

Ice harvesting in Manchester. Blocks of ice packed away in sawdust were preserved for use in the warm months. *Courtesy Norman Grimason*

Spruce Street Saloon, at the corner of Birch and Spruce streets, Manchester, circa 1903. *Courtesy Olive Finnegan Montovani*

W.K. Smith & Company, on the corner of Village Street and Connecticut Boulevard, East Hartford, circa 1900. *Courtesy East Hartford Historical Society*

George Stanley Lumber dealer wagon, Andover, circa 1900. *Courtesy Bolton Town Clerk's Office*

Cheney Bros. blacksmith shop, Manchester. *Courtesy Manchester Historical Society*

Ann, John, Frank and Joe Scheibenpflug set up a stand to sell honey, Manchester, 1915. Anna Scheibenpflug is watching from the porch.
Courtesy Norman Grimason

Peter Larson's Saloon, Charter Oak Street, Manchester, 1906. Behind the bar: John Sexton, Larson's cat, "Andre" and Peter Larson. Others, unidentified.

Courtesy Manchester Historical Society

Business block in East Hartford, circa 1908. *Courtesy East Hartford Historical Society*

Woodbridge Tavern, Manchester Green, 1910. *Photo courtesy Thelma Woodbridge*

Marshall Osella delivering ice in Manchester, circa 1910. *Courtesy Arlyne Ansaldi*

Milk delivery wagon in front of John Knoll's store, Manchester, circa 1910. *Courtesy Norman Grimason*

Wet and Wash Laundry delivered laundry to area residents twice a week. The business was on Maple Street in South Manchester. *Courtesy Manchester Historical Society*

Interior of the Wet and Wash Laundry on Maple Street, South Manchester. *Courtesy Manchester Historical Society*

F.T. Blish Hardware Company employees take a moment to pose for the photographer in 1910. The business was located on Main Street, Manchester.

Courtesy Manchester Historical Society

Cheney Brothers head office building during World War II, flies the Minute Man Flag, awarded for War Bond sales, and the Army Navy E flag for production excellence in aiding the war effort. *Courtesy Manchester Historical Society*

Roman Schiller and Joe Scheibenpflug inspecting bee hives at 194 School Street, Manchester, 1915. *Courtesy Norman Grimason*

The Good Candy delivery truck was quite the conversation piece, with a chicken on top. *Courtesy Norman Grimason*

Cars line up this street in Hebron for Wallace White's Auction, May 3, 1916. The Record Building is on the right.
Courtesy Donald Robinson

Oakland Paper Mill in Manchester as seen looking south across the pedestrian bridge from the mill pond on the Hockanum River in the early 1900s.
Courtesy Mark S. Sutcliffe

Popular Barber Shop, J.J. Keating Proprietor, at 1085-1087 Main Street, Manchester, circa 1917. *Courtesy Manchester Historical Society*

Paul B. Hagedorn at his Flats Filling Station on Tolland Turnpike east of Oakland Street, Manchester, circa 1920. *Courtesy Mark S. Sutcliffe*

Organ grinder entertains children in front of John Knoll's store at 165 School Street, Manchester, circa 1918. "Mutter" Knoll is the lady sitting on the steps. *Courtesy Norman Grimason*

Aerial view of Cheney Brothers silk mills in Manchester, which during the firm's glory days, from the 19th century through the 1930s, was Manchester's largest employer by far. *Courtesy Manchester Historical Society*

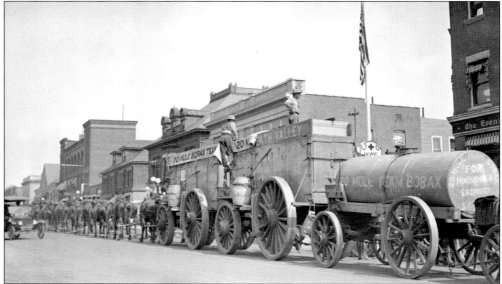

G. Clayton Campbell worked as a meat cutter for Campbell's Quality Grocery in North Manchester, 1918. *Courtesy Morgan Campbell*

Borax's famous 20-mule team, used as a promotion, visited Manchester in 1920. *Courtesy Norman Grimason*

Farm House Chocolates, Route 31, opposite Lisicke Beach, Wamgumbaug Lake, Coventry, circa 1920. *Courtesy Coventry Historical Society, Helen Beville Collection*

Interior of Farm House Chocolates, opposite Lisicke Beach, Wamgumbaug Lake, Coventry, 1920. *Courtesy Coventry Historical Society, Helen Beville Collection*

Employees Bob Newcomb (top) and Charles McCarthy (right) worked for Erving Campbell who owned Campbell's Quality Grocery, North Manchester, 1918. *Courtesy Morgan Campbell*

Burnside Mill, East Hartford, circa 1920. *Courtesy East Hartford Historical Society*

Ayer gas station on Daley Road, Route 31 corner, Coventry, 1922. Fred, Wolcott and Lloyd Ayer are posing for photographer. *Courtesy Coventry Historical Society, Bill Ayer*

Robert Schubert Shoe Repairing at 3 Summer Street, Manchester, circa 1925.

Courtesy Carol Sutcliffe

The Popcorn Man, Manchester, 1920s, had a gas-fired popcorn machine that also produced steam for a whistle which he used to alert the customers that he was in the neighborhood. *Courtesy Norman Grimason*

In the 1920s, Joe Scheibenpflug was in the soda business with Fred Sobielo (far left in the photo). Soda sold for 5 cents a bottle plus 2 cents deposit.

Courtesy Norman Grimason

The Frisbie Company, was the largest pie producer in Connecticut. They were famous for their individual 5 cent pies. Their antique trucks, this one shown in Manchester in the 1920s, were in use until about 1950, when the company went out of business. *Courtesy Norman Grimason*

Manchester Dairy ice cream truck, driver and children and their dog in front of John Knoll's store on School Street, 1920s. Notice the dog is trying to eat the ice cream. *Courtesy Norman Grimason*

Valvoline Oil delivery truck in Manchester, 1920s. *Courtesy Norman Grimason*

Placing of the store sign at John Knoll's store, Manchester, 1925.
Courtesy Norman Grimason

Pero Fruit Stand at 276 Oakland Street, Manchester, 1927. *Photo courtesy Charlie King*

Interior of Campbell's Quality Grocery which operated at Depot Square in North Manchester from 1917-1931. The owner was Erving Pinney Campbell. Photo, 1928. *Courtesy Morgan Campbell*

Spanish-American War Veterans at the State Theater, Manchester, 1937.
Courtesy Andrew Hall

Manchester Motor Sales (Oldsmobile dealer) and Amoco Gas, East Center Street, Manchester, 1930. *Courtesy Manchester Historical Society*

FARM & HOME

Agriculture has only gradually surrendered its hold on our towns to the housing projects and industrial development that have slowly swallowed up more and more of the open space in Manchester, Andover, Bolton, Coventry, East Hartford, and Hebron during the past 100 years.

Every decade, the older people among us say, there are more structures and fewer fields.

Oh, there are still working farms in every town, but we don't encounter farmers hard at work every day.

In addition, the process of farming has changed dramatically since the old days. Technology has improved our efficiency dramatically and has replaced powerful horses with horsepower.

Make no mistake: Farming was a hard life from the turn of the century through the 1950s all right, as some of the pictures in this chapter show. We see a Coventry farmer working with his oxen, laborers haying in Bolton, a Hebron farmer caring for his orchard while atop a horse-drawn wagon, and a Manchester woman bringing in her corn harvest.

Carpenter Homestead, North Coventry, 1890s. Ralph M. Carpenter holding horse "Tom." Nancy, his wife, standing in front of door. *Courtesy Bill Ayer*

Edgar Colman and another man with their oxen-drawn wagon, late 1800s.
Courtesy Coventry Historical Society

Residence of Reverend F. B. White, Andover, late 1800s. He was born in this house in 1866. *Courtesy Andover Historical Society*

Haying in Bolton, circa 1900. *Courtesy Bolton Town Clerk's Office*

One of the oldest houses in Bolton, early 1900s. This was formerly the White Tavern on the corner of Brandy and Bolton Center Road.
Courtesy Eleanor and Norman Preuss

Strong house, Hebron Road, Bolton, 1900. It was one of the oldest houses in the town. *Courtesy Eleanor and Norman Preuss*

Wright residence, Hebron, circa 1905. *Courtesy Clifford Wright*

Fogil Homestead in Gilead, Hebron. *Courtesy Hebron Historical Society*

Residence on Darlin Street, East Hartford, circa 1901. *Courtesy East Hartford Historical Society*

Otto Senkbeil, left, unidentified man and Charlie Schiller at an abandoned farm house in Bolton, circa 1920. *Courtesy Norman Grimason*

Log cabin in Bolton, circa 1910. *Courtesy Norman Grimason*

Gleason's moving day, School Street, Manchester, 1916. *Courtesy Norman Grimason*

H. Randall Tennant, spraying his apple trees, Church Street, Hebron.
Courtesy Hebron Historical Society

Caroline Knoll, known as "Mutter" with corn harvest at 163 School Street, Manchester, 1915. *Courtesy Norman Grimason*

Bunce House at 34 Bidwell Street, Manchester, built in 1834.
Photo courtesy Nancy Andrusis

PEOPLE

This chapter features a wide variety of portraits of individuals who live in or who once lived in our towns.

In the pages ahead, we are presented with the images of babies and toddlers, teen-agers, young men and women, mothers and fathers, and older folks.

And we see them involved in a wide variety of social situations: a grandfather horsing around with his grandson, a family setting out together for a winter walk, a woman wearing her mother's gown on her wedding day, some girls out boating, and a couple dancing at a senior prom.

Of course, we also see many families and individuals in a more typical portrait situation: posing for formal photos that friends and relatives, along with future generations, will cherish.

As their last names reveal, these individuals come from a wide variety of ethnic backgrounds. But it's interesting that our ability to identify with the experiences surrounding their photos testifies to the success of the melting pot in making us all similar, all Americans.

Scheibenpflug family and Schubert family at 194 School Street, Manchester, 1923. *Photo courtesy Carol Sutcliffe*

Keeney Hutchinson, Bolton, 1897. *Courtesy Norman and Eleanor Preuss*

Ida Douglas, Hebron, late 1800s. *Courtesy Alberta Hilding*

Eleanor Maxwell Hutchinson, Bolton, 1896.
Courtesy Norman and Eleanor Preuss

Alphonse, Mary, Ralph, and Walter Wright, in front of their home on Burrows Hill Road, circa 1897.
Courtesy Clifford Wright

Alice Daniels Fargo and her husband Charles, East Hartford, early 1900s.
Courtesy East Hartford Historical Society

Libbie and Chauncey Hollister, early 1900s. *Courtesy East Hartford Historical Society*

Robert Schubert family, South Manchester, circa 1908. Elizabeth, Anna, Max, Bernhard, Robert and Robert Schubert. *Photo courtesy Carol Sutcliffe*

"Mutter," "Vater," and son, John Knoll prepare for winter in Manchester, 1915. John is tripping the shutter with a string attached to his foot. *Courtesy Norman Grimason*

Anna K. Scheibenpflug and her children at Center Park on Memorial Day, circa 1915. *Courtesy Norman Grimason*

Grimason family at 198 Eldridge Street, Manchester, circa 1918. Sam, May, Joe, Martha, Mrs. Sarah, Norman, Mr. James Grimason. The empty chair is for Jim who was in the Army during World War I. A service flag is overhead. A blue star indicated a family member was in the service and a gold star meant a serviceman was killed in the war. *Courtesy Norman Grimason*

The Scheibenpflugs in front of their home at 194 School Street, Manchester, 1915. The parents, Joseph and Anna, then the children, Anna, John, Josie and Frank. *Courtesy Norman Grimason*

Organ Grinder at 163 School Street, Manchester, 1915. *Courtesy Norman Grimason*

Keeney Hutchinson, Bolton, 1917. *Courtesy Norman and Eleanor Preuss*

"Vater" taking cow to "cow lots" on Autumn Street in Manchester, 1920. Mr. McGurie owned a cow pasture east of Autumn Street in Manchester. He charged a few dollars a month for pasturing a cow there. These cows were led there each day, then brought back to their own barns for the night. *Courtesy Norman Grimason*

Miss Adelia Loomis of Bolton receiving an award, circa 1919. For a time, she served as a post mistress and librarian in Bolton. *Courtesy Bolton Town Clerk's Office*

Clarissa Pendleton with Eleanor Lord wearing her mother's 1893 wedding dress.
Courtesy Donald Robinson

Family photo in front of Mr. and Mrs. W. C. Robinson's Route 66 Post Hill home, 1920s. Back row: Jennie Leonard Robinson, Cousin Millie Robinson, Nancy Robinson Porter. Front row: William Clifford Robinson, Horace Welton Porter.
Courtesy Donald Robinson

William E. Burke and Hattie Burke who lived at 21 Cambridge Street, Manchester, 1920s. *Photo courtesy Craig R. Johnson*

Everett G. Lord shows his grandson Donald how to ride the goat and sulky, Hebron Green, 1932. *Courtesy Donald Robinson*

Albina Raccagni sitting on a Model-T Ford, owned by Enrico Gaggianesi.
Courtesy Albina Raccagni

Oleksinski family and neighbors at 21 Kerry Street in front of a bakery in Manchester, circa 1934. *Photo courtesy Virginia Narkon*

Peter F. Sasiela of Manchester when he was 24 years old in 1936. *Courtesy Roseanne Sasiela*

Arlyne Belle Richardson, daughter of Ernest and Bernice Richardson, Manchester, 1945. *Courtesy Arlyne Ansaldi*

Albina Raccagni in a victory garden at 68 Woodbridge Street, Manchester, June 29, 1943. *Photo courtesy Albina Sasiela*

Norm Grimason (front) and his brother, Ed Grimason, president and vice president respectively of the "School Street Rent-A-Goat Company." *Courtesy Norman Grimason*

Norman Narkon and Virginia Oleksinski at the Senior Prom, Manchester High School, 1949. *Photo courtesy Virginia Oleksinski*

Jeanette Richardson and Barbara Prior of South Manchester, 1946.
Courtesy Arlyne Ansaldi

"Best friends" Samuel I. Richardson and granddaughter Arlyne B. Richardson with the chickens at the backyard coop at 69 Oak Street, Manchester, 1946.
Courtesy Arlyne Ansaldi

SOCIETY

As the photographs on the following pages show, religion was a key component of life in earlier days in Manchester, Andover, Bolton, Coventry, East Hartford, and Hebron.

In any of these towns, no matter where you went, you were never far from the sight of a steeple or the sound of church bells.

But churches were not the only social gathering points.

In days past, residents were closer to the land. There were many more farms in our towns than there are today. Even people who lived in the more heavily settled areas of town had agriculture on their minds: They cultivated gardens or raised chickens out back.

Thus, it comes as no surprise that those with agricultural interests were drawn together by their shared interest, and the grange was one outlet.

Music also was a common interest, as the photos in this chapter of bands and a glee club attest.

Members of the Bolton Juvenile Grange No. 6, circa 1907. *Courtesy Bolton Town Clerk's Office*

Victorial Congregational Church, built after the fire in 1882. *Courtesy Donald Robinson*

First Congregational Church, Coventry. This church is the second structure, built, circa 1854. The first building, built in 1712, was destroyed by fire. Photo, circa 1870. *Courtesy Coventry Historical Society, Helen Beville Collection*

Baptist Church, Andover, late 1800s. *Courtesy Andover Historical Society*

Methodist Church, Coventry, early 1900s.
Courtesy Coventry Historical Society, Ethel Crickmore Harris collection

A view up School Street, South Coventry with St. Mary Catholic Church in the distance. *Courtesy Coventry Historical Society*

St. John's Episcopal Church, East Hartford, early 1900s. *Courtesy East Hartford Historical Society*

South Coventry Sunday School picnic, circa 1905. *Courtesy Coventry Historical Society*

Congregational Church, Andover, circa 1900. *Courtesy Andover Historical Society*

Interior of the Bolton Congregational Church, 1911. The church was decorated for Bolton Center School's graduation. Notice the daisies and ferns hanging down from the chandelier. *Courtesy Bolton Town Clerk's Office*

Interior of St. Mary Church on School Street, South Coventry, early 1900s. *Courtesy Coventry Historical Society*

Military band, South Manchester. *Courtesy Manchester Historical Society*

On Sunday afternoons, people used to go for walks in town and gather to sing barbershop. In this photo this group is in front of Reiser Store on Clinton and School streets in Manchester, circa 1915. *Courtesy Norman Grimason*

Manchester Pipe Band. *Courtesy Manchester Historical Society*

Members of the Nutmeg Racing Pigeon Club, 1933. Most of the members were from Manchester. James McKee is in the back row, fourth from left. *Courtesy Norman C. McKee*

South Coventry Brass Band, circa 1910.
Courtesy Coventry Historical Society, Herman Le Doyt, Sr. collection

Bolton Congregational Church. *Courtesy Bolton Town Clerk's Office*

Third anniversary of Societa 'Femminile of Manchester, 1938.
Courtesy Louise Piantaneida

Glee Club, directed by Al Pearson, Manchester. *Courtesy Andrew Hall*

TRANSPORTATION

Efficient public transportation was a benefit of life in many Connecticut towns during the first half of the 20th century.

But it came at a cost - one paid in terms of dollars and sweat.

The photographs on the following pages indicate how much hard, heavy work went into projects like constructing a road in Andover or a bridge in Bolton Notch.

Improved transportation benefited everyone. Better roads helped prevent problems like the one encountered by auto drivers who needed horses to pry their vehicles out of mud holes.

And expanding trolley and railroad lines, shown operating in several towns, made traveling convenient and relatively inexpensive for the majority of individuals, most of whom did not own automobiles.

Travel by air, however, remained a novelty that was more exciting than it was practical.

Barnstormers, like those shown in a photo contained in this chapter, could ignite a youngster's imagination, or even an old-timer's, but people who wanted to complete a long journey invariably went by rail.

Out for a ride around Hebron in Chester Tennant's 1910 Stanley Steamer, September 19, 1910. Children: Allyn and Doris. Adults: Chester, Harry and wife, Annie Tennant Rathbone. *Courtesy Donald Robinson*

Stage coach in front of what is believed to be the first Hebron Post Office and Charles Post general store, circa 1875. *Courtesy Alberta Hilding*

Mr. and Mrs. William Baldwin, Coventry, late 1800s. *Courtesy Coventry Historical Society*

Old toll bridge from East Hartford to Hartford. It was built in 1818 and burned in 1895. *Courtesy Louis V. Mueller*

Freight headed west toward Manchester from the Bolton railroad station, late 1800s. Photo taken from Bolton Notch. *Courtesy Bolton Town Clerk's Office*

Railroad gang, Bolton Notch, circa 1900. *Courtesy Bolton Town Clerk's Office*

Trolley line in South Coventry opposite Nelson Bearce home, late 1800s.
Courtesy Coventry Historical Society, Mrs. Rufus Munsell collection

Trolley terminal,
Manchester Green,
early 1900s.
Courtesy Thelma Woodbridge

Railroad yard in Bolton, early 1900s. *Courtesy Eleanor and Norman Preuss*

Train coming through a cut at Bolton Notch, early 1900s.
Courtesy Eleanor and Norman Preuss

Marvin Howard carting freight for Bolton Soap Works, Bolton, circa 1900.
Courtesy Bolton Town Clerk's Office

Steels Crossing, Bolton, circa 1900. Those in the photo: Loren Metcalf, Harry Milburn, Jim Conners, John Massey. *Courtesy Bolton Town Clerk's Office*

Turnerville Railroad Station, now the Amston section of Hebron, circa 1900.
Courtesy Alberta Hilding

Horses, "Prince and Kit" who belonged to Calvin Hutchinson, transport George Wippert (front) and George Alvord around Bolton, just below Steele's Crossing, circa 1900.
Courtesy Eleanor and Norman Preuss

Lacon Robertson's bus, used to carry passengers from the railroad depot to South Coventry Village in the early 1900s.
Courtesy Coventry Historical Society

Special trolley to Laurel Park, possibly for a Sunday School picnic, circa 1910.
Courtesy Morgan Campbell

Construction of Bunker Hill Road Bridge, Andover, circa 1910.
Courtesy Andover Historical Society

Construction of Bunker Hill Road Bridge, Andover, circa 1910.
Courtesy Andover Historical Society

Construction of Bunker Hill Road Bridge, Andover, circa 1910.
Courtesy Andover Historical Society

Manchester Train Depot at North Manchester. *Courtesy Manchester Historical Society*

View of North Manchester railroad depot, circa 1910. Here train service from the outside world connected with the Cheney family's short railroad line that carried freight and passengers across town to South Manchester. *Courtesy Manchester Historical Society*

Henry Molson and his wife, Linda Kulpinsky Molson, on an Indian motorcycle in front of their home at 216 School Street in Manchester, circa 1920. Linda was a practical nurse in a nursing home in Hartford. During a Christmas season a tree decorated with electric lights started a fire which led to her death. As a result, a Connecticut state law was passed banning electric lights on live-cut trees in public buildings. *Photo courtesy Norman Grimason*

Railroad station at Bolton Notch, circa 1913. *Courtesy Dick Symonds*

Southern terminus of South Manchester Railroad, 1910. With 2.25 miles of track, the SMRR was once the shortest privately owned railroad in the United States. It was created by the Cheney family to connect their silk mills with the east-west trunk line through the north end of Manchester. *Courtesy Louis V. Mueller*

Train from Andover arriving in Bolton before the construction of the bridge.
Photo courtesy Norman Grimason

John Knoll and Ella Hager at Bolton Notch before construction of the bridge. *Photo courtesy Norman Grimason*

Bridge construction begins at Bolton Notch. *Photo courtesy Norman Grimason*

Bridge construction at Bolton Notch. *Photo courtesy Norman Grimason*

Bridge construction at Bolton Notch. *Photo courtesy Norman Grimason*

Bridge construction at Bolton Notch. *Photo courtesy Norman Grimason*

Railroad crew, Bolton, circa 1900. *Courtesy Bolton Town Clerk's Office*

Horses were used to help get automobiles out
of the mud, Manchester, circa 1915.
Courtesy Manchester Historical Society

Early auto converted into a house on wheels, Coventry, circa 1920.
Courtesy Coventry Historical Society, Helen Beville Collection

Early auto converted into a delivery wagon with an advertisement for Davis art metal
corner for hip roofs, Coventry, 1920. *Courtesy Coventry Historical Society, Helen Beville Collection*

On Sundays, former World War I pilots used the cow fields, owned by Mr. McGuire, for "barnstorming" shows, charging five dollars a ride. Anna and Frank Scheiben-pflug squeezed into a one seater for the last ride of the day for a tour over Manchester, a "two-for-one" deal. *Courtesy Norman Grimason*

Main Street, looking north, South Manchester, 1920s. *Courtesy Manchester Historical Society*

William E. Burke, Connecticut Company motorman on the Manchester Hartford trolley, 1920s. He lived at 21 Cambridge Street, Manchester. *Courtesy Craig R. Johnson*

Railroad station in Bolton, circa 1920. *Courtesy Eleanor and Norman Preuss*

DISASTERS

Heavy winds and rain combined to cause monumental damage in New England during the fabled Hurricane of 1938, perhaps the worst natural disaster in the region during the 20th century.

Due to its location on the Connecticut River, East Hartford suffered severe flooding, some of the effects of which are shown in the photographs on the following pages.

The hurricane struck New England on Sept. 21, 1938. Since severe rains earlier in September already had caused some streams to flood, the hurricane's downpour elevated water levels to far above flood stage.

A different kind of wreckage resulted in Manchester at 1:46 a.m. on Oct. 14, 1933, when the "Bullet," a fast freight train running between Portland, Maine, and New York City, plunged off the tracks.

Derailed locomotives and cars snapped poles, fence posts, and trees, and compacted themselves into a tangled mass of steel. Incredibly, no one was seriously injured in the crash.

Flooding on Connecticut Boulevard, East Hartford, 1938. *Courtesy East Hartford Historical Society*

It was early in the afternoon of October 13, 1913, when pupils of Miss Wood's third grade class in Room 23, on the second floor of the old wooden Ninth District School, Manchester, first saw smoke in the hall. The teacher wouldn't allow the children to leave the room for the fire escape until the fire bell rang. Miss Bennet was the principal. She knew that a group of girls were taking showers in the basement and that they were unaware of the fire. Going through the smoke and fire to warn them, her hair and face were burned. She was awarded a necklace of gold beads for her bravery. Later, the Bennet School was named for her. *Courtesy Norman Grimason*

High water on Darlin Street, East Hartford, April 9, 1901. *Courtesy East Hartford Historical Society*

Wreck of the west-bound "Bullet" at Apel's crossing 1:46 a.m. October 14, 1933, Manchester. *Courtesy Manchester Historical Society*

No one was hurt during the wreck of the west-bound "Bullet" in front of Apel's Opera House at 1:46 a.m. October 14, 1933, Manchester. This freight train was carrying shoes and lobsters. *Courtesy Norman Grimason*

This automobile had a hard time getting around East Hartford after the hurricane in 1938. *Courtesy East Hartford Historical Society*

View around East Hartford, after the 1938 hurricane. *Courtesy East Hartford Historical Society*

Flooding in front of the South Green Tavern (right), after the 1938 hurricane, East Hartford. *Courtesy East Hartford Historical Society*

Hurricane damage near South Street, Manchester, 1938. *Courtesy Joseph L. Czerwinski*

Flooding on Connecticut Boulevard, East Hartford, 1938. *Courtesy East Hartford Historical Society*

RECREATION & CELEBRATION

Seen from a modern perspective, the leisure activities of local residents 50 to 100 years ago must be labeled as simple pleasures.

They're activities that most of us have done, or could easily do. Things like fishing with a pal, group bicycling, picking berries in the country, boating, and spending a sunny afternoon listening to music.

Instead of modern amusement parks with their death-defying rides, our parents and grandparents might ride a trolley to a park that offered activities like a merry-go-round ride.

Team sports like baseball also were popular. And, of course, movie-going was as big decades ago as it is today, if not bigger.

Winter may have curtailed many of those activities, but it offered compensation in the form of sledding and ice-skating.

When it came to celebrations, parades seem to have been a favorite. Manchester parades on Armistice Day and for special celebrations honoring the homelands of local immigrants and the town's centennial are depicted.

Walter Senkbeil, left, and his friend Howard Flavell have been out fishing and are proudly showing their catches in front of John Knoll's store, Manchester, 1920s. *Courtesy Norman Grimason*

Trolley celebration at the Lakeside Pavilion, South Coventry, early 1900s. *Courtesy Coventry Historical Society*

Summer cottage built by Miss Carrie Eldridge on a plot of land purchased from Mrs. Maryette Hutchinson. Professor Samuel M. Alvord and Mrs. Alvord are pictured in this group. *Courtesy Eleanor and Norman Preuss*

Social on the Green, believed to be across from Patriot's Park, Coventry, early 1900s. *Courtesy Coventry Historical Society, Ethel Crickmore Harris collection*

Bicycle Club, Coventry, organized by Charles Coombs and John Chaplain, early 1900s.
Courtesy Coventry Historical Society, Ethel Crickmore Harris collection

Boating on Willimantic River, Coventry, early 1900s.
Courtesy Coventry Historical Society, Ethel Crickmore Harris collection

Berry pickers at Steele's Crossing, Bolton, 1906. *Courtesy Bolton Town Clerk's Office*

Chester Tennent's Baseball Nine, Hebron, 1908. Left to right, back row: Arthur Kelly, Rob Cobb, Cyrus Pendleton, Chester Tennent, Fred Rathbun, Arthur Jacqueth, Frank Smith, Ed McMurry. Front row: Edward Miner, John Lyman, Fitch Jones, Dana Jacqueth. *Courtesy Donald Robinson*

Armistice Day Parade down Main Street, Manchester, in front of Magnell's Drug Store, 1918. *Courtesy Norman Grimason*

Lizzie Stoddard, Minnie Alexander and Emma Arnweius, East Hartford, early 1900s. *Courtesy East Hartford Historical Society*

In 1913, the Circle Theatre was revamped from a temporary store built by the House family after their store burned in Manchester. This, the "old Circle" was originally known as "The Home of Silent Drama" then after façade changes it became known as "The World in Motion" as seen here in the mid-teens. In 1920, this building was razed and replaced by the "New Circle Theatre," which took up the back end of the House and Hale building. *Courtesy Norman Grimason*

Man running the projector at the Circle Theatre in Manchester, circa 1913. *Courtesy Norman Grimason*

Coventry men's baseball team, 1908. Mavin Clark's Team. *Courtesy Bill Ayer*

Hebron Baseball Team, 1908. Left to right, back row: Everett Frink, Frank Smith, Dana Jacqueth, Arthur Jacqueth. Front row: Fitch Jones, John Lyman, Bert Lyman, Ed Miner, Cyrus Pendleton. *Courtesy Donald Robinson*

Children heading for a Sunday School picnic in North Manchester, circa 1910. *Courtesy Morgan Campbell*

Merry-go-round at Laurel Park, Manchester, circa 1912. *Courtesy Norman Grimason*

Group posed for the photographer during Dr. Cyrus H. Pendleton and Mary Welles 50th wedding anniversary celebration in Hebron, 1916. *Courtesy Donald Robinson*

Watkins Brothers Baby Carriage Parade, March 27, 1915, Manchester. The Watkins Brothers Furniture Store was at the right of the photo, at the corner of Main and School streets, later relocated to the corner of Main and Oak streets. In the center of this photo is Magnell's Drug Store and Ice-cream Bar; a large ice cream cone was a nickel. To the left is a barber shop and a harness shop at the corner of Eldridge Street. *Courtesy Norman Grimason*

John Knoll went on Sunday afternoon walks with the local boys to stage photos such as this one at a lumber mill on Birch Mountain, 1917. In the photo are: Hugo Lautenbach, in the far back, Joe Ramondo, to his left, other two unknown. Charlie Schiller is ready for the saw as Norman Grimason, Sr., far right, looks on. *Courtesy Norman Grimason*

"Heights Gang" sits on what is called the Rickety Bridge near Oak Grove Street, circa 1920. *Courtesy Norman Grimason*

Sledders enjoy the snow in Manchester, 1920. *Courtesy Norman Grimason*

Skating on the reservoir in Manchester, 1920. *Courtesy Norman Grimason*

Boaters enjoying an afternoon on Wamgumbaug Lake, Coventry, circa 1920. *Courtesy Coventry Historical Society, Helen Beville Collection*

Young girl in a foot race at West Side Oval, Manchester. *Courtesy Norman Grimason*

Warehouse Point contingent marching in Manchester's Homeland Day celebration on June 13, 1914. *Courtesy Stanley Dynia*

Anna Howarth Prentice (center) with sisters, Katie and Susie Howarth having their afternoon tea in Manchester, circa 1918. *Courtesy Norman Grimason*

Whiskey operation at Bolton Lake, circa 1918. Those identified: Bill Senkbeil, Hugo Lautenbach and Dutch Senkbeil. *Courtesy Norman Grimason*

South Manchester Fire Department Hose and Ladder Company No. 4 showing off their American LaFrance ladder truck in Manchester's Centennial Parade, October 1923. *Courtesy Norman Grimason*

Diving and swimming at Globe Hollow, circa 1925. *Courtesy Norman Grimason*

Albina Raccagni dressed in costume for a Manchester parade, 1930s.
Photo courtesy Albina Sasiela

Sunday afternoon at Lakeside Pavilion, South Coventry, circa 1920.
Courtesy Coventry Historical Society

Firemen marching in the Manchester Centennial Parade, October 1923.
Courtesy Norman Grimason

Children marching in the
Manchester Centennial
Parade, October 1923.
Courtesy Norman Grimason

State Theater staff, Manchester, 1934. Jack Sanson, right front. *Courtesy Andrew Hall*

Sledding at 255 School Street in Manchester, 1936. *Courtesy Norman Grimason*

Cast of "Kiddies Revue" directed by Jack Sanson, at the State Theater, Manchester, 1935. Music was by Sam Kaplan, "Orchestra of Hartford." *Courtesy Andrew Hall*

Trade School Baseball team, circa 1936. *Courtesy Manchester Historical Society*

Coventry men's baseball team, 1948. Back row: Manager Walt Thorp, Joe Sumara, Buds Gagnon, Johnny Leigher, Don "Gabby" Geer, Buster Beaumont, Joe Flint Vanderbuilt, Lefty Woodworth. Front row: Harman Cochrene, Lou Hadded, Leo Morris, George Hinkle, Jake LeDoyt, Fred Rose, Charlie Hawkins. Casey Jones, bat boy.
Courtesy Coventry Historical Society, Bill Ayer

Italian float in front of Howell Cheney Technical School on School Street, Manchester, 1930s. Albina Raccagni, the second from left. Ermano Garaventa created the float. *Photo courtesy Albina Sasiela*